Praise for Juliann Mangino's

ABCs for Daddy!

"I wish I had had an easy-to-read and concise book like this when my wife, Ruth Ann, and I raised our two sons."

Dr. Jon Wefald
President, Kansas State University
1986 to 2009
and a parent of two sons, Skipp and Andy

"As a parent of two young boys, every new day is a reminder of my enormous responsibility to raise kind, compassionate, tolerant, and loving children. ABC's for Daddy! is loaded with simple, yet powerful, messages that will help me on my parental journey. A 'must read' for every dad in America!"

Chad Foster, best-selling author of
Teenagers Preparing for the Real World

Build positive character traits with

ABCs for Daddy!

Part of the *Young Parenting Series*

ABCs for Daddy!

Part of the *Young Parenting Series*

Created and written by
Juliann G. Mangino, Ed.D.

ISBN-13: 978-0-615-58218-4

Doc Publishing

Table of Contents

Acknowledgements

ABCs for Daddy! is dedicated to the many fathers who bond with their children early; change diapers; read bedtime stories; soothe their crying child; talk to their infant; sing with their toddler; read and learn about parenting and child development and always respect their child's mother.

My own father continues to be a source of my inspiration through his light-hearted attitude and love of life. He is a wonderfully caring father to five children, thirteen grandchildren and two great-grandchildren.

Matthew, my husband, began his fathering during my pregnancy with our twins. Melina and Mark are active twelve-year-olds and Matthew continues to impress me with the knowledge and interest he holds in continuing to be the most supportive and understanding father I know.

Walk a Little Slower Daddy
Author: Unknown

"Walk a little slower Daddy,"
said a child so small,
"I'm following in your footsteps
and I don't want to fall.

Sometimes your steps are very fast,
Sometimes they're hard to see;
So walk a little slower, Daddy,
For you are leading me.

Someday when I'm all grown up,
You're what I want to be;
Then I will have a little child
Who'll want to follow me.

And I would want to lead just right,
And know that I was true,
So walk a little slower, Daddy,
For I must follow you."

Introduction

Family values are passed from generation to generation. Fathers play a key role in shaping and developing family values through the building of positive character traits—one at a time.

Everyone has character traits, both good and bad. As you begin to cobble together an individual's character traits—what emerges is that person's personality.

We want our children to grow up understanding the importance and value of dignity, fortitude, achievement, and generosity, to name a few. Positive character traits, if used on a consistent basis, can improve academic success, weed out bullying, improve relationships, and more.

Family values define the whole system of beliefs that will guide your children throughout their lives. To teach family values and positive character traits is to raise a child who will make a positive contribution to society.

ABCs for Daddy! is second in the *Young Parenting Series* and focuses on a father's role in building and developing character in the lives of his children. *ABCs for Daddy!* explores one positive character trait for each letter of the alphabet. Each positive character trait is showcased with a quote and a short sketch of the person quoted. Each of the 26 quotes and accompanying sketches are meant to provide inspiration.

According to Healthy Teen Network, active parental involvement early in a child's life helps to form a positive parent-child bond and sets the foundation for a healthy parent-child relationship.

Young fathers play a crucial parenting role. Research suggests that children who grow up without fathers may be at greater risk for poverty, behavior and achievement problems at school, teen pregnancy, dysfunctional relationships, involvement in the criminal justice systems, aggressive behaviors, and victims of violence or abuse.

ABCs for Daddy! serves as a meaningful resource for use in group or individual meetings with fathers. This book can also be used alone as a self-help working journal for the young father. Additionally, the two books from the *Young Parenting Series, ABCs for Mommy!* and *ABCs for Daddy!* provide inspiration for both parents working together to establish a strong value system that enhances their relationship with each other and their children.

Each positive character trait presented is followed by an exercise to enhance and review the learned trait. The exercises are provided to prompt you, as a young father, to reflect on how best to apply the character trait. The exercises are useful tools that encourage dialogue and enhance your understanding of the material presented.

Additionally, there are word puzzles, nursery rhymes, Clear and Unclear Messages to help you effectively communicate with your children, "recipes" for fun, fatherhood website addresses, journal pages, suggested readings for fathers, and suggested readings for fathers to share with their children.

Give Clear Messages to Your Child

Describe:

- **Who**—"you and your brother"
- **What**—"screamed"
- **When**—"just now"
- **Where**—"at the dinner table"

ABCs for Daddy!

A is for **Achievement**—
both personally and professionally.

B is for **Bold**—
dare to be.

C is for **Change**—
the one constant in life.

D is for **Dignity**—
hold onto it.

E is for **Empathy**—
work to understand the feelings of others.

F is for **Fortitude**—
to have the strength to move forward.

G is for **Giving**—
of yourself to others.

H is for **Humble**—
use modesty in your behavior and attitude.

I is for **Imagination**—
never hold back from dreaming.

J is for **Joy**—
in the pleasures of life.

K is for **Kindness**—
> share some with a warm smile.

L is for **Logical**—
> think it through.

M is for **Mature**—
> be it in your actions, spoken and unspoken.

N is for **Nutritious**—
> eat healthy and stay healthy.

O is for **Optimistic**—
> be the positive thinker.

P is for **Partner**—
> fathering is a partnership.

Q is for **Question**—
> don't hesitate to ask.

R is for **Respect**—
> yourself and others.

S is for **Strength**—
> we gain over time.

T is for **Tireless**—
> using energy and desire.

U is for **Understanding**—
> your feelings and emotions.

V is for **Values**—
>   create your family values and stick to them.

W is for **Wisdom**—
>   gained through knowledge and experience.

X is for **X Chromosome**—
>   the letter that makes your daughter unique.

Y is for **Yield**——
>   slow down and take notice.

Z is for **Zany**—
>   show your child your fun side.

A is for **Achievement—** both personally and professionally.

"It is not the going out of port, but the coming in, that determines the success of a voyage."

~Henry Ward Beecher~

Henry Ward Beecher was a prominent Congregationalist clergyman, social reformer, abolitionist, and orator in the mid to late 19th century. An advocate of women's suffrage, temperance and Darwin's Theory of Evolution, and an opponent of slavery and bigotry of all kinds (religious, racial, and social), Beecher held that Christianity should adapt itself to the changing culture of the times.

Each week, thousands of worshipers packed Beecher's Plymouth Church in Brooklyn. Abraham Lincoln was in the audience at one sermon, and poet Walt Whitman visited Beecher's church as well. Mark Twain went to hear Beecher and described the pastor as "sawing his arms in the air, howling sarcasms this way and that, discharging rockets of poetry and exploding mines of eloquence, halting now and then to stamp his foot three times in succession to emphasize a point."

Every so often we should all reflect back on our successes and achievements. Often times, it is something that took a great deal of courage or ability to complete. Every time you succeed at something that you have worked for, savor the achievement— you've earned it.

It will be difficult to move toward a new goal if we never stop to recognize our past accomplishments. With every achievement you make, you are building new skills and abilities that add to your character as a person.

As a parent, we should continue to strive to improve our lives through personal and professional development while also encouraging our children to be the best they can be and recognizing their efforts along the way.

Children will model your conduct and lifestyle. If they observe someone who takes pride in setting goals and working towards reaching those goals, then they too will become goal setters.

Power Lesson for Achievement

List a few of your achievements.

A._____

B. _____

C. _____

Describe what efforts it took to achieve these.

A._____

_____

B. _____

_____

C. _____

_____

B is for **Bold**— dare to be.

"Be bold and courageous. When you look back on your life, you'll regret the things you didn't do more than the ones you did."

~H. Jackson Brown, Jr.~

H. Jackson Brown, Jr. is an American author best known for his inspirational book, *Life's Little Instruction Book*, a *New York Times* bestseller. *Life's Little Instruction Book* was the first book to ever simultaneously occupy the number one spot on the *New York Times* bestseller list for both paperback and hardback.

Brown's books have been translated into 35 languages and have sold millions of copies worldwide. They have spawned calendars, posters, clothing, greeting cards, audiocassettes, screensavers, and even fortune cookies. Brown has also received thousands of letters from readers all over the world. Their content ranges from the simple, "I enjoyed your book and I read a page or two every night before I go to bed" to the humbling, "Your book convinced our family to adopt a special needs child."

It takes a bold person to acknowledge fear and stand strong. As a young father, through the journey of raising your child, you may find yourself in situations where you need to take a stand and express your opinion or thoughts.

As you make the transition into fatherhood, there will be times when bold and decisive action will be required when your child's health and well-being are at stake. This may include decision-making regarding child care, preschool, choice of family doctor, or even play dates.

It is your duty to participate in those decisions. Do not hesitate to do what you believe is right and just, for you, your family, and the people important in your life.

When it comes to your child's well-being, be firm but respectful. Listen carefully to all available options, seek the guidance of those you respect, but – most importantly – make a decision with your child's best interest at heart.

Power Lesson for Bold

When have you had to take a stand and express yourself clearly to achieve something?

Academically or professionally?

_____

_____

Regarding your son or daughter?

_____

_____

Other times?

_____

_____

Clear Message:

Tell children what needs to be done in a few words.

Then show and describe how to do it.

C

is for **Change**—
the one constant in life.

"Change is the law of life. And those who look only to the past or present are certain to miss the future."

~John F. Kennedy~

John F. Kennedy was the 35th President of the United States, serving from 1961 until his assassination in 1963. Before he was elected to congress and then the U.S. Senate, he was a war hero. His book, *Profiles in Courage*, won the Pulitzer Prize.

He was known for his rousing speeches and vision for the future of the country. He talked about putting a man on the moon before the end of the decade and the nation succeeded in 1969.

Although he had big thoughts, he was also aware of the need to improve the lives of the down trodden around the world. To this end he created the "Peace Corps", a volunteer agency that got young Americans around the world to help the needy.

Kennedy came from a well-to-do political

family. His grandfather was the mayor of Boston; his father the U.S. ambassador to England before World War II. His brother, Robert, ran for president in 1968, but he too was assassinated. His brother Edward ran, unsuccessfully, for president in 1980.

There are things in our lives that we can control. Do not focus much time and energy on those things beyond our control.

What changes should we focus on? First, we should look at how we could improve our lives, personal or professional, and begin to make transformations, one at a time. It is not an impossible task.

As a father, the way you spend your personal time is a gradual but necessary change. Perhaps you will want to spend more quality time with your children. That may require you to spend *less* time socializing with friends. A commitment to being a responsible father has to be done consciously and purposefully.

In order to change a negative behavior, or to strengthen an area in your life, you need to commit to the change. By being committed, you must be willing to allow time necessary for the change to take effect. If you do this, before long you will see that you have incorporated quite a few positive changes that will have a direct impact on your family and more importantly on your children.

Power Lesson for Change

Name three things you would like to change, or improve, as a father? (for example: *learn patience* or *read about parenting techniques*)

1. _____

2. _____

3. _____

Would you like your child's life to be the same as yours or different? Why?

_____

_____

Which experiences do you wish you had had as a boy?

_____

_____

D is for **Dignity**— hold onto it.

"Dignity does not float down from heaven it cannot be purchased nor manufactured. It is a reward reserved for those who labor with diligence."

~Bill Hybels~

Bill Hybels is the founding and senior pastor of Willow Creek Community Church in South Barrington, Illinois, one of the most attended churches in North America, with an average attendance of nearly 24,000 as of 2011.

The church has been consistently listed as one of the most influential churches in America. The ranking comes from Hybel's peers and other pastors from around the country. He is the founder of the Willow Creek Association and creator of the Global Leadership Summit. Hybels is also an author of a number of Christian books, especially on the subject of Christian leadership.

Everyone should be treated with love and respect regardless of race, gender, economic status, education, religion, or any other divide.

However, dignity is self-respect or self-worth. Everyone is worthy of respect. Dignity begins with poise and self-respect.

Dignity is pride in yourself. How you view yourself will direct how well you take care of yourself, and that will reflect your idea of self-worth. Simply put, if you don't like or respect yourself, how will you be productive and effective in relationships with other people?

Dignity goes beyond self-worth. Family dignity is a joint effort of family pride in the family's past, present, and future; professional dignity is pride in your career choice; educational dignity is the pride you feel regarding your education, training and skill development choices you've made in life and have put into action.

Power Lesson for Dignity

I define DIGNITY as _____

_____

_____

List three things that have brought dignity into your life:

1. _____

2. _____

3. _____

Unclear Message:

Telling your child, "You were good at the mall."

You need to *explain* the good behavior and what you mean by "good."

Tell your child, "I liked the way you were quiet while I spoke with the salesperson."

E is for **Empathy**— work to understand the feelings of others.

"How far you go in life depends on you being tender with the young, compassionate with the aged, sympathetic with the striving and tolerant of the weak and the strong. Because someday in life you will have been all of these."

~George Washington Carver~

George Washington Carver was a scientist, botanist, educator, and inventor who rose to fame in the late 19th and early 20th century. He was born a slave during the Civil War.

Carver's compassion shined in his work with poor farmers to grow alternative crops. He experimented with crops like peanuts, both as a source of their own food and as a source of other products, to improve the lives of peanut farmers.

He developed and promoted about 100 products made from peanuts that were useful for the house and farm including cosmetics, dyes, paints, plastics, gasoline, and nitroglycerin. He received numerous honors for his work, including the Spingarn Medal of the NAACP.

In 1941, *Time* magazine dubbed him the greatest African–American scientist alive.

Sympathy and empathy are two of the most commonly misunderstood terms. Sympathy is a shared emotion. Sympathy exists when the feelings or emotions of one person is shared by similar feelings in another person. It is usually the sharing of unhappiness or suffering.

On the other hand, empathy is the ability to imagine oneself in another's place—to be able to understand the feelings, desires, ideas or actions of another. An actor must have the ability to empathize in order to play a specific part in a movie or play.

We need to exercise the art of empathizing in order to understand the feelings and emotions of others. Our children will often require us to empathize in order to understand how they must feel when something doesn't go quite right or when they cannot master a new skill.

Putting yourself in "someone else's shoes" is an attempt to understand their situation or feelings. There is a simple question that we can ask ourselves as a way to exercise the art of empathy—"How would I feel?" Put yourself in someone else's shoes on a daily basis until you get a feel for how to empathize and how this new way of understanding can help you become a better man.

As a way to ensure that you have the understanding of empathy, imagine that someone you love is suffering. Try to imagine their pain and anxiety with as much detail as possible. After doing this exercise a few times, try moving on to imagining the suffering of other people you encounter. How has that suffering shaped their relationship with you and other people?

Power Lesson for Empathy

For the next week, exercise the art of empathy daily by describing a situation and how you empathized with that person.

Sunday: _____

_____

Monday:_____

_____

Tuesday _____

_____

Wednesday:_____

_____

Thursday: _____

_____

Friday:_____

_____

Saturday: _____

_____

F is for **Fortitude**—
to have the strength to
move forward.

"Just because today was a terrible day, doesn't mean tomorrow won't be the best day of your life. You just have to wake up and get there."

~Pete Wentz~

Pete Wentz plays the bass and writes songs for his band *Fall Out Boy*. Wentz is not just a music man; he is also a businessman. He owns his own record label, Decaydance Records; a clothing company, Clandestine Industries; a film production company, Bartskull Films; and a nightclub called Angels & Kings. Wentz makes every day a good day.

He doesn't just make money; he also gives it away. His philanthropic activities include collaborations with Invisible Children, Inc. and UNICEF's Tap Project, a program that helps bring clean drinking water to people around the world.

Of course, it would be great if everything went just the way we planned it. If all good things happened with no obstacles, barriers or challenges for us to face, life would be easy—almost too easy. But the everyday happenings often require us to find the strength necessary to handle those unexpected stressors.

Whether it be at home, school, work, or play, there will always be opportunities for us to make good choices and move forward. We will constantly be tested to see that we have the fortitude or strength to prove to ourselves, and others, that we can continue to move forward.

There are times when you may need to reach out to others who will emotionally support you when you are facing difficult challenges. That emotional support could be exactly what you need to get through the rough times.

Remember: pay it forward. When someone close to you is having a tough time, make yourself available; offer a shoulder to lean on.

Power Lesson for Fortitude

Complete the statements below:

As an expectant father, I am (or was) challenged by the thought of:

_____

_____

As a new father, I am challenged by the thought of:

_____

_____

As a friend, I am challenged by the thought of:

_____

_____

When I am faced with an unexpected tough time, I will exercise fortitude and make every attempt to:

- Evaluate the situation

- Find emotional support through friends or family

- Move forward with a plan

_____

Your initials of commitment

Journaling

Journaling is a written form of creative expression.

Journal writing is an excellent way to explore your goals, dreams, accomplishments, and memories.

There are many styles of journaling, from structured, or guided writing, to a specific travel journal. For the purposes of this book, it is recommended that you use a freestyle approach to journal writing. Freestyle journaling is the art of using a blank journal page and letting your thoughts flow freely while you write them on paper.

This book includes six Journal Pages to be used as you work your way through the book. You will have ample opportunities to document your feelings, thoughts, and opinions.

Throughout this book, when you turn to a **Journal Page**, take the time to write out your thoughts. It will soon become natural, and you may learn that journaling can help you deal with important issues in your life in a thoughtful way.

You need to develop a written action plan that will get you on your way to a fulfilling and productive day. To get you started, I've included a single "prompt" on each Journal Page. The prompt is a simple statement, "Today, I will _____ in order to feel fulfilled." Happy Journaling!

G

is for **Giving**—
of yourself to others.

"The most important thing is this: to be able at any moment to sacrifice what we are for what we could become."

~Charles Du Bos~

Charles Du Bos was a French literature critic whose writings on William Shakespeare and Lord Byron helped bring English literature in the consciousness of the French people. Du Bos was willing to sacrifice his esteem with the French as he introduced his countrymen to the subtleties of English literature.

Du Bos was exposed to English literature at an early age because of his mother's English ancestry. He studied at a prestigious English university.

His chief interest was in what he called the "soul" of a work and its effects in the "soul" of a reader. He understood that works of literature could have a profound effect on the reader. He viewed the understanding of literature essential to the well-being of society.

When we hear the word "giving," our first thought might be of handing someone in need a few dollars or dropping some coins in a donation bucket. However, giving is more than a financial commitment. It is about reaching out to our family, friends, and neighbors and making the effort to give of ourselves in various ways.

It is admirable that you donate impulsively to someone who asks for help, but we should also work on giving purposefully. To give purposefully means that you planned to give because you believed in the efforts and because you *wanted* to give.

Giving should become a habit, and to give freely—without expecting anything in return except for the good feeling you've created within yourself—is the greatest gift to give! When you give of yourself, you are also modeling a very positive behavior for your child to learn and develop.

Generosity comes in many forms—donations of money or goods or the donation of time to help others. Giving will generate a positive feeling. You feel good about yourself and the power you have to help others.

Who knows? You may just inspire the person you help to give of themselves, and the web of giving will continue to expand.

Power Lesson for Giving

Reflect back on the past few months: How have you given of yourself? Perhaps you helped someone load bagged groceries in her car or donated your gently-used clothing to a secondhand store. Think back and list a few moments of giving—no matter how big or how small.

My Giving Chart

Giving Challenge:

Work to recognize moments when we can give of ourselves in order to help others.

Clear Message:

Correct children when
they've made a mistake,
and help them learn
from it.

H

is for **Humble**— use modesty in your behavior and attitude.

"Talent is God-given. Be humble. Fame is man-given. Be grateful. Conceit is self-given. Be careful."

~John Wooden~

John Wooden is arguably the best basketball coach that ever lived. The "Wizard of Westwood," as he was known, won ten NCAA national championships in a 12-year period as head coach at UCLA. His teams won a record 88 consecutive games. He was named National Coach of the Year six times.

As a player, Wooden was the first player to be named All-American three times, and he was part of a team that won a national championship. Wooden was named to the Basketball Hall of Fame as a player and a coach, the first person ever enshrined in both categories.

Wooden was renowned for his short, simple inspirational messages to his players. These messages were often a road map to success in life as well as in basketball. Wooden certainly knew the difference between what was God-given, man-given, and self-given.

To be humble one must be ready to accept his shortcomings, acknowledge others' talents and accomplishments, learn from their own mistakes, and be willing to learn from others.

Humility can be difficult to teach and, at times, even more difficult to model. This is because when you model humility, it is often done with subtlety and, therefore, not easily recognized.

The most important aspect of being humble is that you are completely honest with yourself. Accept yourself as you are and be open to improvement and change.

There are many benefits to being humble. Humility allows you to be more satisfied with your life, helps you get through the tough times, helps you become an effective learner, and can improve your relationships with others.

Be proud of your accomplishments, and don't be afraid to share those successes with others. It's not bragging if you talk about yourself and others in a passionate and genuine way—"Look at what *we* achieved." It is equally important to be a good "reporter"—that is, ask questions and *listen* to responses.

Finally, be gracious and thankful. Don't hesitate to express your appreciation.

Power Lesson for Humble

Excerpt from *Ten Ways to Be More Humble*

1. Use the response, "It's my pleasure," when someone thanks you for doing something.

2. Use the response, "I'd be honored," when someone asks you to help them.

3. Listen more than you talk.

4. Give credit for other's ideas.

5. It's OK to be wrong, so admit it.

6. Admit when you don't understand or know something.

7. Recognize your talents as gifts, not your own ability.

8. Share your own knowledge, and pass on what you have learned.

9. Value other people's time as much as your own.

10. Don't boast about your achievements—let others recognize them instead.

Children Learn What They Live

If a child lives with criticism, he learns to condemn.

If a child lives with hostility, he learns to fight.

If a child lives with ridicule, he learns to be shy.

If a child lives with shame, he learns to feel guilty.

If a child lives with tolerance, he learns to be patient.

If a child lives with praise, he learns to appreciate.

If a child lives with fairness, he learns to have faith.

If a child lives with approval, he learns to like himself.

*If a child lives with acceptance and friendship, he
learns to find love in the world.*

~Dorothy Law Nolte~

Key Points when giving clear messages:

1. Position yourself at eye level with your child.
2. Make eye contact with your child.
3. Use a calm voice.
4. Be aware of your facial expressions and body language.
5. Eliminate distractions.

Journal Page

Today, I will _____
in order to feel fulfilled.
DATE_____

_____
_____
_____
_____
_____
_____
_____
_____
_____
_____
_____
_____
_____
_____
_____
_____
_____
_____
_____
_____
_____
_____
_____
_____
_____

I

is for **Imagination**—
never hold back from dreaming.

"All successful people, men and women, are big dreamers. They imagine what their future could be, ideal in every respect, and then they work every day toward their distant vision, that goal or purpose."

~Brian Tracy~

Brian Tracy is an author and motivational speaker. After dropping out of high school, Tracy got a job as a merchant sailor and traveled around the world for eight years. He eventually visited more than eighty countries on five continents!

After his nautical adventures, Tracy became a successful businessman. He serves as Chairman of Brian Tracy International, a human resource company doing business in the United States and thirty-one other countries.

In 2009, Forbes Magazine reported that Tracy's books and seminars make about $25-30 million a year. Even without a high school diploma, Tracy could imagine a future of success—imagine what you can do

We all dream. As toddlers, we dream and imagine what we can do with a new toy. As a boy, you might have dreamed of being a firefighter or a football player.

To dream and imagine is what drives us to accomplish a task, complete a project and begin new adventures.

A simple daily journal is an easy way to keep focused of a goal that you imagine—dream big—write it down. When you shoot for the stars, your journal will be your road map to getting there.

Use a simple notebook, write the date, and begin jotting your thoughts. You can go a step further and have a specific "dream journal" or "goal journal" to record your thoughts and progress.

As fathers, you have a great deal to dream about and imagine with your son or daughter. Imagine yourself teaching your child how to dream through play, and work to make that dream a reality. Imagine yourself as a role model and go out and be that role model for life.

Power Lesson for Imagination

Do…Allow yourself quiet time each day to simply think and dream.

Do…Try writing in a journal for one week to sort your thoughts and determine if journaling can help you stay focused on your dreams. Begin with the Dream Journal on the next page.

DREAM Journal Page

DATE_____

_____
_____
_____
_____
_____
_____
_____
_____
_____
_____
_____
_____
_____
_____
_____
_____
_____
_____
_____
_____
_____
_____
_____
_____

I imagine accomplishing _____.

J

is for **Joy**—
in the pleasures of life.

"Grief can take care of itself, but to get the full value of a joy you must have somebody to divide it with."

~Mark Twain~

Mark Twain was the pen name for Samuel Langhorne Clemens. Twain was an American author and humorist. He is most noted for his novels, *The Adventures of Tom Sawyer,* and its sequel, *Adventures of Huckleberry Finn.*

Twain grew up in Missouri. He first apprenticed as a printer. He worked as a typesetter and contributed articles to a newspaper. After working as a printer in various cities, he became a riverboat pilot on the Mississippi River.

He later failed as a gold miner, so he finally turned to journalism. He achieved great success as a writer and public speaker. His wit and satire earned him praise from critics and peers, and he was a friend to presidents, artists, industrialists, and European royalty.

Having someone to share life's joys with is a special blessing. When something humorous or pleasant happens through the course of a day, often your first thought is "who can I share this great story with."

It is wonderful to have family close and to have special friends to share your mutual joys. That is why it is important to choose your friends carefully. They can have a lasting, important influence on your life.

What are the pleasures in life? As a new father, there will be many opportunities to share your joy— learning the gender of your baby, graduation from school, a new job opportunity, your child's latest developmental achievement and, of course, the fun things children do and say.

Power Lesson for Joy

- Share your joys and SMILE every day!

- Think about it—have you smiled today?

  What made you (or makes you) smile?

  _____

  _____

- Have you made someone smile today?

  How did you (or will you) create joy for someone else?

  _____

  _____

K is for **Kindness**— share some with a warm smile.

"And as I've gotten older, I've had more of a tendency to look for people who live by kindness, tolerance, compassion, a gentler way of looking at things."

~Martin Scorsese~

Martin Scorsese is a movie director, screenwriter, producer, actor, and film historian.

He was the descendant of Italian immigrants. As a boy, he had asthma and couldn't play sports or do strenuous outdoor activities with other kids. His parents and older brother would often take him to the movies. It was in the theater that Scorsese developed his passion for cinema.

He won the Academy Award for Best Director for *The Departed* in 2006. He was nominated five other times. His movies include cinematic classics like *Taxi Driver* in 1976, *Raging Bull* in 1980, and *Goodfellas* in 1990.

What does it mean to be kind? Does it mean you are a pushover or soft? Is it that you simply know how it feels to accept kindness so you offer it back in return?

One reason to work on being kind—it makes us happy and brings happiness to those around us. Kindness is contagious. It is difficult to be coy or rude to someone who is showing you compassion and kindness.

You may need to do a self-assessment—how are you projecting yourself in order to determine if you are offering kindness and compassion to others?

It is important to make sure we are not always centered on ourselves and our own happiness. Exuding kindness and compassion often mean setting aside our needs and putting others needs or wants before our own.

Compromise is not a sign of weakness. Compromise will show your interest in reaching a resolution that is not 100% in your favor—but also not a total loss.

It is easier to offer kindness when you have a better understanding of the other person's situation. Instead of recognizing the differences between yourself and others, try to recognize what you have in common. The Power Lesson that follows will help you quickly evaluate a person and begin to recognize your commonalities rather than your differences.

Power Lesson for Kindness

When you meet new people, discreetly go through the following steps to help you better see the commonalities you share and ignore the differences that could keep you from sharing kindness and compassion.

Move through the 5 steps with your attention focused on the new person. With each step, tell yourself:

Step 1:
"Just like me, this person is looking for happiness."

Step 2:
"Just like me, this person would like to avoid suffering."

Step 3:
"Just like me, this person has had rough times."

Step 4:
"Just like me, this person is looking to fill his needs."

Step 5:
"Just like me, this person is constantly learning about life."

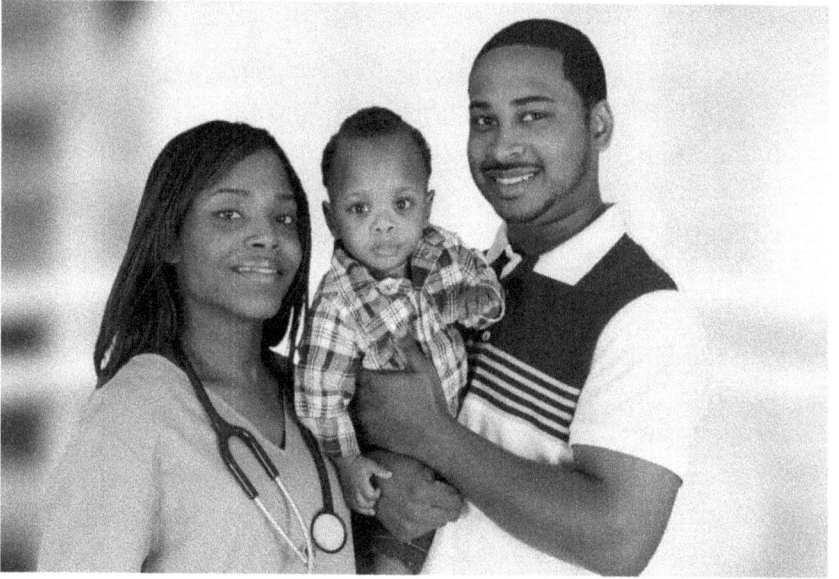

L is for **Logical**— think it through.

"Logic is the anatomy of thought."

~John Locke~

Locke was an English philosopher and physician. He was born long ago in 1632 and lived to become one of the most influential people in England and, perhaps, one of the most influential people of the 17th century.

He would earn the title *father* of liberal philosophy. His ideas would also be used as a keystone for American independence and was often referred to as leaders prepared for the American Revolution and separation of the colonies from England.

Logical thinking is the process where one uses reasoning consistently to come to a conclusion. Logical thinking allows you to reject the quick answers such as "I don't know" or "this is too difficult." It is important to take the time necessary to sort out the situation and details so that you may come to a logical or thoughtful conclusion or solution.

In a bygone era, every street corner had its sage—a philosopher of sorts. In one rough and tumble ethnic neighborhood, the street corner sage would tell all who would listen, "Think about it, and think about it again."

That odd but simple phrase is the essence of logic.

To think logically is to analyze a situation so you can make the best decision possible with the information you have available. This analysis may mean that you need to take some extra time to discuss the details with others you trust or to write down the facts for easier review. Logical thinking includes:

- Having a clear goal
- Planning out what we know to help us reach our goal
- Allowing us to use information to organize and sort out details
- Using reasoning
- Checking conclusions

Once you learn to think—and think again—you'll understand that a quick "I don't know" or "this is too difficult" is simply a lazy mind. A logical mind will pause, think and respond.

Power Lesson for Logical

You will use logic to guide you through the next big decision. Whether the decision is buying a car, renting an apartment or deciding on a college, you should sort out the details and make a logical decision.

A. Write down the goal or decision to be made.

_____

B. List any facts or details.

_____

_____

C. Discuss with others.

D. List pros and cons of various decisions.

_____

_____

E. Review your conclusions.

F. Make a logical decision and stick with it (based on your research).

_____
Logical decision written here.

M is for **Mature**—be it in your actions, spoken and unspoken.

"Maturity is knowing when to be immature."
~Randall Hall~

Hall is a classically trained musician. However, Hall didn't pursue a career playing the saxophone with a symphony orchestra. Instead he played with the Rock 'n Roll band Lynyrd Skynyrd.

Hall is also a composer. He has become one of the leading performers and composers for cutting-edge music for saxophone. He is also an Associate Professor of Music at Augustana College.

Maturity comes with age and experience. In our early teens, we begin to think and process information differently. During this crucial time in our lives, we make decisions that can impact the rest of our lives.

Maturity is how you choose to manage your life and responsibilities.

There are different types of maturity. Webster's Dictionary defines maturity as "full grown and developed." Intellectual maturity is when you are able to care about your personal well-being. A person who considers others' feelings is showing social maturity.

With intellectual maturity, you are able to follow instructions and be open-minded in various situations. This may pose a challenge on occasion. At work or at school, you may be asked to complete a task using specific tools or instructions that you are unfamiliar with. It is up to you to use your intellectual maturity to work through the task.

Social maturity is what enables us to work and interact with others in social settings. To be socially mature offers the chance to show some humility when necessary. A socially mature person may offer to help someone without acknowledgement. You help because you *want* to help—that demonstrates maturity.

Maturity is built over time. To mature in age is a natural process. To mature intellectually and socially takes work. Those men who want to be socially and intellectually mature must be willing to always look for ways to improve and to react to life's everyday problems with grace and dignity.

Power Lesson for Mature

Maturity comes with experience.

Adult decisions require maturity.

Time helps to develop maturity.

Understanding others takes maturity.

Responsibilities are managed when mature.

Engage with others in a mature way.

Unclear Message:

Telling your child, "You're driving me crazy!"

Note: They won't understand the meaning.

N

is for **Nutritious—** eat healthy and stay healthy.

"Those who think they have no time for healthy eating will sooner or later have to find time for illness."

~Edward Stanley~

Stanley, also known as the Earl of Darby, was educated at the top English schools, Eton College and Oxford. After graduating, he pursued a life in public service. He held various public positions until he was elected a Member of Parliament. He held the seat in the House of Commons until 1906.

Stanley died at the age of 80 in September 1907.

___

We all know that health food is necessary for growth and development as well as our overall well-being. Food is also an important part of our relationship with others. We eat and prepare foods in order to celebrate and socialize.

Research on the relationship between family and food has shown that well-functioning families have better overall health and well-being than poorly functioning families.

K.E. Rhee wrote in *Pediatrics* journal, "When families are not functioning well, parents, children, and others are at an increased risk for poor nutrition, being overweight, or developing other health-related problems like diabetes."

There are a few rules of thumb that can be used to balance the amount and quality of foods that families eat.

1. **Don't prompt your children to eat.** Prompting your children to eat their vegetables may actually discourage them from eating these foods.

2. **Don't use food as a reward.** It actually causes the food used as the reward to be more desirable and the food that was required to eat becomes less desirable.

3. **Don't restrict access to food.** This sometimes causes the child to actually eat more of that food when it is available.

4. **Model healthy food behaviors.** You have a powerful influence on food choice and preferences in your children. Children raised in homes with more available fruits and vegetables

often have greater preferences for these foods.

Remember, families who eat together, stay together. Meal time is an important time to share your day and your plans for the future.

Power Lesson for Nutritious

Practice these 5 recommendations in order to improve your family's health and nutrition.

> **Stay away from pressure.** Instead of pressuring your child to eat, try to offer food in an open-ended manner, such as, "Would you like more to eat?" This gives the child the option to either take more or refuse.

> **Don't use food as a reward.** Create situations where the healthier foods are more appealing. "Dress up" the vegetables with a healthy dipping sauce or have them help you make a healthy trail mix.

> **Avoid restricting food.** Offer healthy snacks at set times that will still allow them to be hungry by dinnertime so that they will be more likely to eat the prepared meal.

> **Model good behavior.** If you are excited about eating healthy foods, then your children will be too.

> **Allow them to have a voice.** By including the child in some of the healthy food choices and purchases, you are empowering them to have control over their eating and health.

Journal Page

Today, I will _____
in order to feel fulfilled.
DATE_____

_____
_____
_____
_____
_____
_____
_____
_____
_____
_____
_____
_____
_____
_____
_____
_____
_____
_____
_____
_____
_____
_____

Crossword Review
A-N of
ABCs for Daddy!

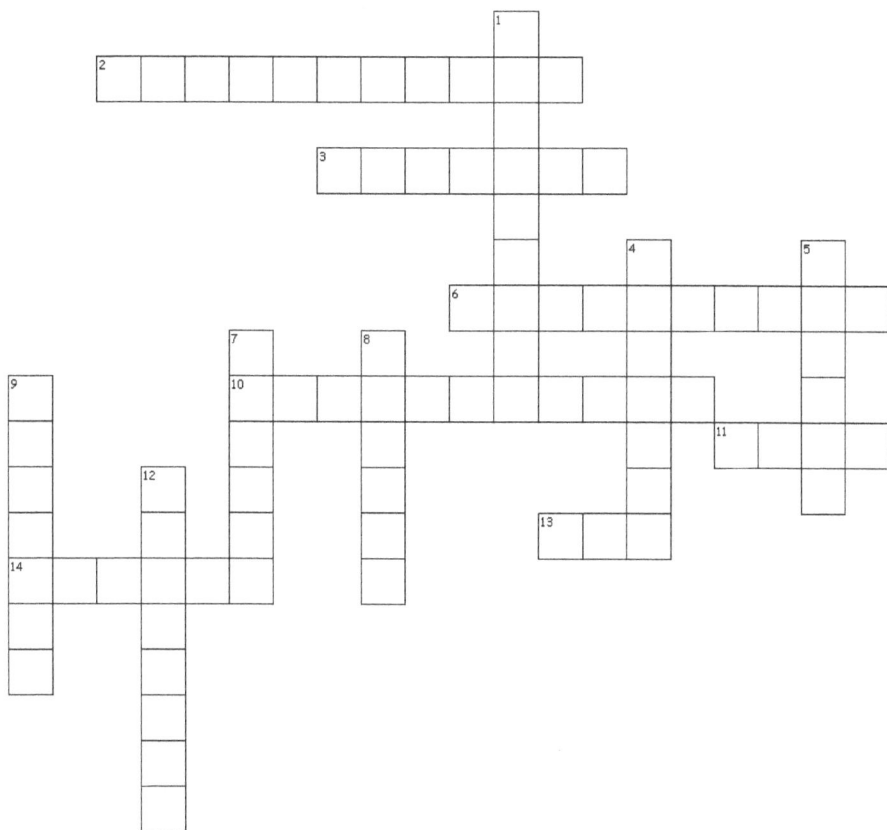

Across

2. Use this to keep dreaming
3. To understand the feelings of others
6. Eat healthy and stay healthy
10. You should strive to reach this both personally and professionally
11. Dare to be
13. The pleasures of life gives you this
14. This is the one constant in life

Down

1. To have the strength to move forward
4. Be sure and hold on to this
5. Modesty in your behavior and attitude
7. Show this in your actions, both spoken and unspoken
8. _____ of yourself to others
9. Be _____ and think it through
12. Share this with a warm smile

O

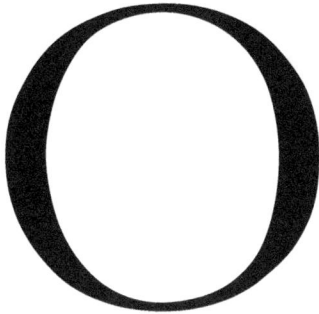

is for **Optimistic**— be the positive thinker.

"We cannot always build the future for our youth, but we can build our youth the future."
~Franklin D. Roosevelt~

Franklin D. Roosevelt was the 32nd president of the United States. President Roosevelt led the nation for more than twelve years. He was elected four times. He lead the nation through two of the trying eras of the 20th century—the Great Depression and World War II.

Roosevelt was a courageous leader, a tireless worker and a tenacious advocate for America. He was also confined to a wheelchair having contracted polio twelve years before being elected president.

Roosevelt was beloved—millions of Americans would sit around their radios during the depression and war to be inspired by his "fireside chats." Roosevelt remains an icon of American culture.

To be optimistic means to take a favorable view of something and to expect a favorable outcome. To think of the positive of situations and events will help you to feel more in control and understand that even the most unfavorable events can have good outcomes. We sometimes need to re-evaluate the situation or look deeper to find the positive side or outcome. Every cloud has a silver lining.

The goal is to be a rational optimist—one who knows that good comes with bad but firmly believes that the good will outweigh the bad. A rational optimist also understands that being pessimistic, or a negative thinker, accomplishes nothing and wastes precious time and energy.

You may need to change your way of thinking about the past and the future as you work towards being more optimistic. Understand that whatever unfavorable event happened in the past does not necessitate that the future will be unfavorable. Past negative experiences help to shape who we are and build character in our lives, making us stronger. Every day is a new day with a new chance to view the world with excitement and joy.

Some tips that will help you incorporate positive thinking with optimism are:

> Use quotes. There are many in this book, to remind yourself to be optimistic.
> Look happy. When you look happy you begin to feel happy.
> Point out to others when you hear someone practicing pessimism and negative thinking.
> Do good things for others.

➢ Recognize that YOU can make a bad situation better.
➢ Count your blessings, focusing on the good things in life.
➢ Avoid people that make you feel pessimistic or unhappy.

Power Lesson for Optimistic

Write positive affirmations, or statements, and hang them in places where you will see them every day such as your bathroom mirror, the refrigerator, in your car, on your computer monitor—you get the idea.

Here are some examples of positive affirmations:

"Anything is possible."
"I can control my attitude towards life."
"I always have a choice."
"My circumstances do not create me, I create my circumstances."

Begin by writing a few positive affirmations here:

_____

_____

_____

_____

Another way to support positive thinking is to write in your journal pages (pp. 43, 66, 87, 97, 123, 135) about how you have made positive changes in the way you view your world.

P is for **Partner**—
fathering is a partnership.

"The most important thing a father can do for his children is to love their mother."

~Theodore M. Hesburgh~

Father Hesburgh is a catholic priest and President Emeritus of the University of Notre Dame. Hesburgh served as Notre Dame's president for thirty-five years (1952–87), the longest serving president in Notre Dame's storied history.

During Hesburgh's tenure at Notre Dame, the institution's endowment grew from $9 million to $350 million, enrollment nearly doubled, and the size of the faculty more than doubled.

As chairman of the U.S. Civil Right Committee in the late 1960s, Hesburgh took courageous positions opposing President Richard Nixon's policies. Those positions ultimately lead to his firing by President Nixon in 1972.

Sometimes, we are able to choose who to partner with for a work project or school assignment. We also have a choice who to partner with in a relationship. When you are about to become a parent, you are in the process of forming a long-lasting partnership with your child's mother. Whether married or single, in the same house or apart, the parenting partnership is one that must be built over time with cooperation and communication as two key components.

In any well-built partnership, each partner contributes their strengths and accepts the other's strengths. For example, mothers and fathers collectively contribute to the raising of a child— perhaps in very different ways. But these varying ways are necessary for successful parenting.

Fathers are more likely to promote a child's intellectual and social development through physical play while mothers are more likely to promote intellectual and social development through talking and teaching during caregiving. The same two developments (intellectual and social) with two different approaches can provide a very balanced approach at parenting.

Fathers tend to be less predictable and more flexible than mothers and have a more physical element where mothers like to follow their routines and patterns with less physical interaction.

Again, two different approaches build healthy relationships, especially when the two parents recognize each other's approach and appreciate their partner's parenting style.

Power Lesson for Partner

Since you are playing on the same team with your child's mother, it is imperative that you communicate effectively and work as a team or partnership.

Use the checklist below to be sure you are a strong partner:

- o **Be respectful.** Respect your child's mother because she is important in your child's life.

- o **Open mind.** Receive what your child's mother is saying and listen attentively with an open mind.

- o **Courteous.** Be courteous and give enough notice of events or changes in your situation that might have implications for your child's mother.

- o **Honesty.** Keep trust in the partnership by being honest to each other.

- o **Communicate.** Keep in touch through written notes or quick texts. It is important for your child to see that both parents communicate regularly.

Clear Message:

Teach your child to think for himself and begin to problem solve.

Q

is for **Question**—
don't hesitate to ask.

"The fool wonders, the wise man asks."
~Benjamin Disraeli~

Benjamin Disraeli was involved in British politics for 40 years. He was twice the Prime Minister of Great Britain during the 19th century. Disraeli's family was of Italian decent and Jewish faith, both unusual backgrounds for high level British officials during the 19th century.

During his decades in politics, Disraeli became embroiled in a long and well-publicized feud with a House of Commons colleague William Gladstone. Disraeli once described the difference between a misfortune and a calamity in this way: "If Gladstone fell into the Thames River, it would be a misfortune. But if someone dragged him out again, that would be a calamity."

Beyond his stinging wit, Disraeli was also known as a literary and social figure. He invented the political novel, of which *Sybil* and *Vivian Grey* are best known.

Why do birds sing? Why do leaves change color? Why does it rain? These are a sampling of questions your children may ask some day. By age three or four, children begin to get very curious and "why" begins just about every uttered sentence.

So, *why* do we hesitate to ask questions when we get older? We may think we know all we need to know; we may feel that we will look weak or ignorant by asking questions, and sometimes, we are just in such a hurry that we don't stop to ask *why*.

We may think we know all we need to know but, in fact, the more you learn the more you realize how much there is to know—without asking "why" we are left to assume an answer. Instead, get accurate information by asking a few questions.

At times, asking a question may seem like an admission that you "don't know." There is nothing wrong with not knowing—it is wrong to press on without finding out. Asking questions is, in fact, a sign of strength and intelligence. Great leaders are constantly asking questions and are always looking for better answers.

There are different types of questions—open and closed. Open questions give the responder the chance to give a broad answer with detailed information. An example of an open question would be "Why do you think this happened?" Open questions often begin with why, how, or what.

Closed questions limit the responder to a one or two word response such as "yes" or "no." An example of a closed question would be: "Was she angry?"

Open questions often begin the conversation allowing you time to listen attentively. The next step in a conversation is to narrow the information down to main points by asking the closed questions.

Conversations flourish with open-ended questions. Conversations wither with closed questions. Make your conversations flourish.

It may take some practice, but asking questions in a friendly, non-threatening way can provide you with valuable information and open up new relationships, too.

Power Lesson for Question

Practice asking more questions in your everyday conversations.

Instead of *telling* someone something, *ask* them a question.

List something you might *tell* someone today:

_____

_____

_____

Now, rephrase the above statement into a question you might *ask* someone:

_____

_____

_____

Remember: Good questions will stimulate, inform and inspire. Questions help us to teach—and to learn.

R is for **Respect**— yourself and others.

"Respect for ourselves guides our morals; respect for others guides our manners."

~Laurence Sterne~

Laurence Sterne lived in London at the time the thirteen American colonies were still a part of the British Empire. During this turbulent period, Sterne was somewhat of a local politician and activist. He was fervently opposed to slavery long before that position was popular in North America.

Sterne was best known as a novelist and clergyman. He knew a lot about morals and manners. His most beloved works were his novels—*The Life and Opinions of Tristram Shandy, Gentleman,* and *A Sentiment Journey Through France and Italy.* He also published many of his sermons and wrote a memoir.

Respect for others, like other character traits, is learned through example. It is not something with which we are born.

As a father, you are in a powerful position to model respect for your children. Children are always observing and emulating the example you are setting. When they see you listen attentively while engaged in conversation, they are seeing you model respect.

When you hold the door for someone or you give up your seat on the bus for an elderly man or a pregnant woman, they are seeing you model respect.

Your words, without a doubt, express respect for others. Saying "please," or "thank you" to a store clerk who helped you models respect for their time and efforts.

Respect is not to be underestimated. It is contagious—random acts of kindness have a way of empowering others to do the same.

Finally, there are other ways to show respect simply through the tone of your voice or your body language. Let's not forget children are watching and hearing everything. A kind voice when speaking to others and polite body language are the first in modeling appropriate behavior.

Power Lesson for Respect

Make a list of disrespectful words and phrases. Replace with compliments, congratulations, and encouragement. See first example.

Disrespectful...	Replace with...
"You only won because your opponent wasn't feeling well."	"Congratulations on your win. You should be proud."

Brainstorm Rules of Respect for your family. I started you off with the first rule.

Our Rules of Respect

1. We will use good manners using a kind voice and polite body language.

Unclear Message:

Telling your child,
"Super job!"

Note: It's a nice compliment,
but she needs to know more
details.

Journal Page

Today, I will _____
in order to feel fulfilled.

DATE_____

_____
_____
_____
_____
_____
_____
_____
_____
_____
_____
_____
_____
_____
_____
_____
_____
_____
_____
_____
_____
_____
_____
_____

S is for **Strength—** we gain over time.

"You have power over your mind - not outside events. Realize this, and you will find strength."

~Marcus Aurelius~

Marcus Aurelius was Roman Emperor from 161 to 180 A.D. He acquired the reputation of a philosopher king within his lifetime. "Alone of the emperors," wrote a Roman historian, "he gave proof of his learning not by mere words or knowledge of philosophical doctrines but by his blameless character and temperate way of life."

During his reign, the Roman Empire had military triumphs, although he was not a tyrant. His writings or meditations are still revered as a literary tribute to a philosophy of service and duty.

When we hear the term "strength", we often think of physical strength. How much we can lift or how far we can run is a measure of physical strength. Fathers not only need physical strength; they also need the mental strength to make good, sound decisions. Mental strength is gained by our experiences successes, struggles, and failures.

Strength is certainly a measure of power. An object's strength would be its level of breakability where your mental strength is the ability to face adversity and continue to make informed decisions that are in the best interest of you and your family.

Having the stamina to overcome obstacles requires having the mental strength to push forward. There will be times when you feel as though you just don't have the courage or strength to move ahead, and it seems the best option is to give up. Giving up will not solve the problem. Giving up is never an option.

Always face your challenges head-on—ready to problem-solve. Make a plan. In order to solve a problem, you need to have a plan—a road map that leads you step-by-step through your problem to a solution.

When you tackle challenges one step at a time you will enjoy mini-success along each step and be eager to move on to the next step. All along, you are gaining strength and building your self-esteem.

Power Lesson for Strength

True or False

1. _____ Strength is only physical power.

2. _____ Fathers need mental strength to make good parenting decisions.

3. _____ There is only one definition of "strength."

4. _____ "Strength" is having the ability to tackle challenges and obstacles.

5. _____ With every life challenge, we are building strength and character.

Check your answers using the box at the bottom right.

Answers: 1. F 2. T 3. F 4. T 5. T

90

If I Had My Child to Raise Over Again

If I had my child to raise all over again,

I'd finger-paint more and point the finger less.

I'd do less correcting and more connecting.

I'd take my eyes off my watch, and watch with my eyes.

I would care to know less and know to care more.

I'd take more hikes and fly more kites.

I'd stop playing serious, and seriously play.

I'd run through more fields and gaze at more stars.

I'd do more hugging and less tugging.

I would be firm less often, and affirm much more.

I'd build self-esteem first, and the house later.

*I'd teach less about the love of power, and more about
     the power of love.*

~Diane Loomans~

Clear Message:

Tell children what they've done WELL rather than always telling what they *didn't* do well.

T

is for **Tireless**—
using energy and desire.

"It does not matter how slowly you go so long as you do not stop."

~Confucius~

Confucius was a Chinese teacher, editor, politician, and philosopher who lived more than 2,500 years ago. The philosophy of Confucius emphasized personal and governmental morality, correctness of social relationships, justice, and sincerity.

Confucius is traditionally credited with having authored or edited many Chinese classics. He championed strong family loyalty. He also recommended family as a model for ideal government. He championed the well-known principle: "Do not do to others what you do not want done to yourself," an early version of the Golden Rule.

Active, steadfast, eager, resolute, energetic, enthusiastic, hard-working, industrious, perky…these are all synonyms of the word tireless. All of these words have a positive meaning. To be described as "tireless" is a very big compliment, indeed.

To be a tireless worker or tireless volunteer or tireless father is to be one who devotes himself with full commitment and enthusiasm.

It is amazing the amount of energy that you can muster when you become a parent. When assuming the role of a parent, it is imperative that you find your inner strength to play, teach, guide, and learn—all with the tireless energy of wanting to do what is necessary to raise a healthy, happy child. A child who, through the years, has watched and observed the tireless energy of his father will too have a work ethic that fosters success and achievement.

It is up to you to find the energy necessary to be your child's first teacher, to instill a sense of character and pride in your child, and to show by example compassion and understanding of others.

Oh, and don't forget to have fun. Do what you like to do, and you will want to tirelessly commit yourself to the effort.

Power Lesson for Tireless

Let's work together to write a short essay describing the attribute of tirelessness.

Use the words below to complete the paragraphs.

active	energy	committed
devoted	spirit	positive	hard-working

Fatherhood is a very big job. It is the most important job you will ever have. Fatherhood demands that you be _____ and _____ to your children and family.

By being physically _____, you will have more _____ to play with your children. As a _____-_____, tireless father, you will build your child's _____, while promoting _____ energy.

Unclear Message:

Telling your child, "You've got a bad attitude!"

Journal Page

Today, I will _____

in order to feel fulfilled.

DATE_____

_____
_____
_____
_____
_____
_____
_____
_____
_____
_____
_____
_____
_____
_____
_____
_____
_____
_____
_____
_____
_____
_____
_____
_____

U is for **Understanding**— your feelings and emotions.

"Understanding is the essence of love."
~Thich Nhat Hanh~

Thich Nhat Hanh is a Vietnamese Zen Buddhist monk, teacher, author, poet, and peace activist.

In 1960, Nhat Hanh came to the U.S. to study at Princeton University, subsequently being appointed lecturer in Buddhism at Columbia University. By then, he had gained fluency in French, Chinese, Sanskrit, Pali, Japanese and English, in addition to his native Vietnamese.

In 1963, he returned to Vietnam to aid his fellow monks in their non-violent peace efforts. He was forced to leave his native Vietnam because of his work to end the Vietnam War. He lives in the South of France travelling internationally hosting retreats and giving lectures.

Nhat Hanh has published more than 100 books, including more than 40 in English. He continues to be involved in international peace initiatives.

To understand is to know how to define something—to be able to explain, with detail, the essences of something or someone.

To understand your feelings and emotions is a whole new world of thought and emotion. It is a time when we need to look within ourselves and really outline what it is that we like about ourselves, admire in others, and what we aspire to be or do.

There are times when the stressors of life can get in the way and make it difficult for us to establish our true emotion to a situation. We may feel frustrated with a particular situation or anxious about one that awaits us, but either way, we must come to terms with our true emotion and not allow these feelings (emotions) to control our actions in a negative way.

Understand that the way we control and handle our emotions will be a guide to how our children handle their emotions.

Power Lesson for Understanding

List the emotion of each of the emoticons below.

_____

_____

_____

_____

_____

_____

V

is for **Values**— create your family values and stick to them.

"What a child doesn't receive he can seldom later give."

~P.D. James~

P.D. James is an English crime writer. She is most famous for a series of detective novels starring policeman and poet, Adam Dalgliesh.

James had to leave school at the age of sixteen to work because her family did not have much money and her father did not believe in higher education for females. She married Ernest Connor Bantry White, an army doctor, and had two daughters, Clare and Jane.

When White returned from the Second World War, he was suffering from mental illness and James was forced to provide for the whole family until her husband's death in 1964.

James began writing in the mid-1950s. Her first novel, *Cover Her Face*, introduced Dalgliesh who was later portrayed in television dramas and movies.

Family is defined as a social unit consisting of parents and the children they raise. Value is worth. Family values are what is honored and respected in *your* family. Family values become the guide posts for raising a family and often become the foundation for how children learn, grow, and function in the world. Have you established family values?

This lesson will help you to explore family values while also begin to establish your own set of family values. Having strong family values is the foundation of a strong, close family. The values you establish are often what is needed when the twists and turns of life don't go quite as planned and you need the support and guidance of family.

Zen Family Habits' website lists the Top 10 Essential Family Values; they are listed below to help you begin to understand the true worth in incorporating family values:

1. *Belonging.* Each member of the family must feel that they are loved, they belong, and they matter.

2. *Flexibility.* The more flexibility you have, the happier your family will be.

3. *Respect.* The only way to earn and keep someone's respect is to first show them respect yourself. Respect extends from the home to school, work, and other social settings.

4. *Honesty.* This is the foundation of a relationship that is meant to last.

5. *Forgiveness.* Forgiving is not the same as saying what was done is okay. Forgiving is an important choice to make and understanding that everyone makes mistakes from time to time.

6. *Generosity.* Being generous doesn't mean simply handing over money to someone in need. It can also include giving your time, love, attention, or even some of your unused possessions.

7. *Curiosity.* Children have natural curiosity. It is important to encourage your children, and yourself, to continue to be curious and to think critically.

8. *Communication.* Failure to communicate can lead to unhappiness and misunderstandings. When people feel they can talk openly about their hopes, dreams, failures, and successes, it is encouraging and strengthens the bond.

9. *Responsibility.* This is learned early on as we teach our children to put the toys away after playing or to feed the dog. Setting out individual responsibilities for family members works to instill responsibility in everyone.

10. *Traditions.* These are what make families unique. Traditions draw people together and create a sense of belonging for everyone. If you don't have traditions in your family—create them!

Power Lesson for Value

Complete this activity with your family. Have each family member draw three columns on a blank sheet of paper or you can use the prepared table on the next page.

First column. Brainstorm a list of all the activities that you value, in any order. The list may include spending time with your children, work, school, exercise, religion, quiet time, being with friends, video games, etc.

Second column. Now arrange the list from your first column in order of priority (most important will be listed first—and so on).

Third column. List the amount of time spent doing this preferred activity on any given day.

Finally, share your lists and discuss the valued activities and how you could better incorporate the most valued, from the prioritized list, into your daily life.

All activities I value	Prioritize the list of valued activities	Actual time spent
1.	1.	
2.	2.	
3.	3.	
4.	4.	
5.	5.	
6.	6.	

W

is for **Wisdom**— gained through knowledge and experience.

"Wisdom is not a product of schooling, but of the lifelong attempt to acquire it."

~Albert Einstein~

Albert Einstein received the 1921 Nobel Prize in Physics. A German-born physicist, he developed the general theory of relativity, one of the two pillars of modern physics.

After completing his education, Einstein spent two frustrating years searching for a teaching post. He finally secured a mundane position in the patent office. He wrote several groundbreaking research papers in his spare time.

In 1933, Einstein was visiting the United States when Adolf Hitler and the Nazis came to power. He did not return to Germany, where he had been a professor. He settled in the United States and became an American citizen in 1940. His great intellectual achievements made the word "Einstein" synonymous with genius.

Throughout our lives, we gain knowledge through our experiences and our education. That is why we often hear about the wisdom of our elders. When we tap into that wisdom, we make better decisions. The opposite of wisdom is folly—all of us will engage in folly—the goal is to limit those situations.

The wisdom we acquire is a deep understanding and realization of people, things and events. The use of acquired wisdom is demonstrated through the ability to make sound decisions that result from a deep understanding of circumstances and situations.

The ability to make wise judgments comes from controlling your emotional reactions so that reason and knowledge prevail in your decision-making.

In summary, researchers in the field of psychology have defined wisdom as the coordination of knowledge and experience and its use to improve well-being. With this definition, wisdom can be measured using the following criteria:

- A wise person has self-knowledge.
- A wise person seems sincere and direct with others.
- A wise person is asked for advice.
- A wise person's actions are consistent with his/her ethical beliefs.

As a father, you should strive to meet that criteria in order to become wiser in the way you think, perceive, and make decisions.

Power Lesson for Wisdom

List 5 words that describe how we can become wiser.
(i.e. education)

1. _____

2. _____

3. _____

4. _____

5. _____

X

is for **X chromosome—** the letter that makes your daughter unique.

"A father who will pursue infant care tasks with ease and proficiency is simply a father who has never been led to believe he couldn't."

~Michael K. Meyerhoff~

Michael K. Meyerhoff, Ed.D., is executive director of a family advisory and advocacy agency.

He graduated from Harvard University. He has authored three books, thirty booklets, and over 100 articles for both parents and professionals; his regular columns have twice been awarded the first-prize citation from Parenting Publications of America and have been awarded a first-prize National Headliners award.

He makes frequent appearances on radio and television shows, including NBC's *Today Show*, and is regularly invited to speak to parent and professional groups throughout the U.S. and Canada.

The genetic chromosome that defines the sex of a baby is determined by the father. Males are born with an XY set of chromosomes and females are born with an XX set of chromosomes. When the two join, only one of their set of chromosome gets passed on to the child. So the females always pass on the X chromosome and the male passes on either the X or the Y.

This section is dedicated to the important role the father plays in raising a daughter. Victoria Secunda writes, "The good father does not have to be perfect. Rather, he has to be good enough to help his daughter to become a woman who is reasonably self-confident, self-sufficient, and free of crippling self-doubt, and to feel at ease in the company of men."

A daughter needs a father—be it a biological father or a father figure—someone she can depend on during all her stages of life. From infancy through the toddler years, elementary school years, middle school, high school and after graduation, there is never a time in a young girl's life when a father or father figure can't have a meaningful impact.

The most important aspect of the father-daughter relationship is providing your best effort and intentions. Mistakes will be made and challenges will be faced, but if you acknowledge mistakes and face the challenges head-on, your contribution to your daughter's upbringing will make a difference.

The enthusiastic pursuit of a solid father-daughter relationship will help to build a strong, mature daughter who can face her own life decisions with confidence and structure.

In the words of an unknown father, "I believe that I am letting my kids see that a man can be tender, sensitive, warm, attentive to feelings, and present, just plain there. That's important to me because I didn't get any of that from my own father, and I am realizing now how much I missed it."

This dad reminds us that fathering is equally important to both the son and daughter—both need the time, commitment, and love from both parents.

Power Lesson for X Chromosome

FACT or FICTION ?

90% of all homeless and runaway children are from fatherless homes.

FACT

40% of all children that exhibit behavioral disorders come from fatherless homes.

FICTION
(More than twice as many—85%)

71% of all high school dropouts come from fatherless homes.

FACT

41% of teenage girls who get pregnant come from fatherless homes.

FICTION
(Twice that—82%)

85% of all youths in prison grew up in fatherless homes.

FACT

33.5% of American children (24.3 million) live absent their biological father.

FACT
(That's 1 out of 3)

Data provided by Fathers and Children Together.

Y

is for **Yield**—
slow down and
take notice.

"Great things are not accomplished by those
who yield to trends and fads and popular opinion."
~Jack Kerouac~

Jack Kerouac was an American novelist and
poet. He attended Columbia University on a football
scholarship. After an injury derailed his athletic
career, he joined the Merchant Marines during World
War II.

A pioneer of the Beat Generation, Kerouac
became an underground celebrity. Along with other
members of the Beat Generation, Kerouac became a
model for the Hippie Movement of the 1960s and
1970s.

Since his death, Kerouac's literary prestige has
grown, and several previously unseen works have been
published. All of his books are in print today, among
them: *On the Road, Doctor Sax, The Dharma Bums,
Mexico City Blues, The Subterraneans, Desolation
Angels, Visions of Cody, The Sea is My Brother*, and
Big Sur.

We all get busy, and life just seems to "get in the way." We seem to be eager to share with others the struggles or challenges we face rather than sharing the successes. We neglect to appreciate the blessings we have and to revel in the successes we achieved.

The character of yielding encourages you to notice your surroundings by slowing down, just a bit, every single day. The time you take to appreciate what you have can come in the form of a few minutes of alone time. That alone time can occur while in the car, on the bus, in the shower, just before bed, or anytime that works with your schedule.

Once you get in the habit of reviewing all the GOOD things in life, you will then begin to spend much less time dwelling on the not-so-good happenings and deal with them in a more productive manner.

You can deal with the challenges in life a bit easier because you realize, through yielding, that you have a great deal to be thankful for and can overcome obstacles if you take them one step at a time.

Power Lesson for Yield

Over the next few days, list (in Column I) how much time you took each day to Yield and reflect. Then list what you thought about and appreciated (in Column II).

An example has been shown for you.

Column I   **Column II**

Time I took to Yield today...	My appreciation thoughts...
Ex. 10 minutes	For my health and my family's health.

Z is for **Zany**—
show your child your
fun side.

"Being an adult can be fun when you're acting like a child."

~MarcandAngel.com~

"Marc and Angel Hack Life" is a website bursting with inspiration and advice. Marc and Angel enjoy sharing practical thoughts on a broad range of topics pertaining to life, productivity, aspirations, health, work, and general self-improvement.

Marc and Angel explain their website like this: "As we react over the past and dream about our future together, we begin to understand who we are and where we intend to go. Our life presses forth as we stumble over the balance of simplicity and extravagant ambition."

Check it out—being a dreamer who is driven and ambitious can be fun!

Think about it. Now that you are a mature young man, you cannot simply begin singing on a bus or skip down the street. That would be silly.

WE all fondly think back to the fun times we enjoyed playing in our back yards or enjoying playground time with our friends. As adults, we sometimes let life get in the way of our enjoyment— our simple pleasures.

As a mother of twins, I had a blast playing with my son and daughter when they were toddlers and elementary school age. They often asked me not to sing too loud or dance too much in public because they were embarrassed. Were they really embarrassed? I always felt as though they secretly admired my zaniness and how I would skip with them to the bus stop.

Zany is a fun word that means to be comical, clownish, or to be a bit eccentric. Sometimes we need to surprise our children with our zany, or uninhibited, side. We need to show them that we can have their kind of fun, too.

Don't forget to show your children some special outside games you played as a child. Teach them the rules of the game and let them imagine you as a kid having fun. Tell them stories of your childhood. Stories will help you reveal to your children that child inside of you.

Always be adventurous with your children allowing them to see that life doesn't have to be so serious. Take the time to laugh every day and remind your child as I do every morning, "make someone laugh today."

When you smile your child smiles—when children smile the world smiles.

Power Lesson for Zany

Can you name some zany, silly, uninhibited things
your mom, dad, or grandparent did?

_____

_____

_____

_____

_____

_____

_____

Journal Page

Today, I will _____
in order to feel fulfilled.
DATE_____

_____
_____
_____
_____
_____
_____
_____
_____
_____
_____
_____
_____
_____
_____
_____
_____
_____
_____
_____
_____
_____
_____
_____
_____
_____
_____
_____
_____

ABCs for Daddy!
A – Z Double-Puzzle

Use the following word box of *ABCs for Daddy!* positive character traits to solve the Double-Puzzle on the following page.

Unscramble each of the clue words.

Then copy the letters from the numbered cells to the same numbered cell found in the secret message.

WORD BOX

ACHIEVEMENT	BOLD	CHANGE
DIGNITY	EMPATHY	FORTITUDE
GIVING	HUMBLE	IMAGINATION
JOY	KINDNESS	LOGICAL
MATURE	NUTRITIOUS	OPTIMISTIC
PARTNER	QUESTION	RESPECT
STRENGTH	TIRELESS	UNDERSTANDING
VALUES	WISDOM	X CHROMOSOME
YIELD	ZANY	

GIINIOTAMNA [puzzle row with boxes, numbered 8]

HAYPEMT [boxes]

BLDO [boxes, numbered 11, 4]

RAETUM [boxes, numbered 24]

TERSECP [boxes, numbered 7]

DSSEKNIN [boxes, numbered 1]

TITOSINRUU [boxes, numbered 3]

DAGESDITNNNUR [boxes, numbered 12]

HENCAMIEETV [boxes, numbered 19]

GYDTINI [boxes, numbered 23]

OYJ [boxes, numbered 20]

DEYLI [boxes, numbered 17]

RENRAPT [boxes, numbered 14]

WODSIM [boxes, numbered 2]

NYAZ [boxes]

TEHRNTGS [boxes, numbered 13]

SOIMTPTICI [boxes, numbered 18]

GECHAN [boxes, numbered 10]

BELUHM [boxes, numbered 6, 5]

LACGIOL [boxes, numbered 16]

VAELUS [boxes, numbered 21]

QINSOETU [boxes]

FOTDIERUT [boxes, numbered 15]

SELTISER [boxes, numbered 22]

X MOOROHESMC [boxes, numbered 9]

GIVGIN [boxes]

[answer key rows numbered 1 | 2 3 4 5 | 6 7 | 8 9 10 | 11 12 13 14 | 15 16 17 | 18 | 19 20 21 22 23 | 11 24]

125

Fatherhood Helpful Links

www.mrdad.com

Savvy solutions for today's connected dads.

www.fatherhood.org

The National Fatherhood Initiative's mission is to improve the well-being of children by increasing the proportion of children growing up with involved, responsible, and committed fathers.

www.fathers.com

National Center for Fathering provides resources designed to help men become more aware of their own fathering style and then work toward improving their skills.

www.just4dads.org

Just4Dads provides legal help and fathers' rights and information for single dads.

www.greatdad.com

Advice for fathers on parenting, dad care, pregnancy care, adoption, child care, and raising kids and teens.

Suggested Readings for Children

Curious Baby Curious George Counting Book
    by H.A. Rey

Fast and Slow: An Animal Opposites Book
    by Lisa Bullard & Gail Saunders-Smith

Growing Up
    by Diane James, Sara Lynn & Joe Wright

Marshmallow Math: Early Math for Young Children
    by Trevor Schindeler

My Teacher Sleeps in School
    By Leattie Weiss

Opposites
    by Melanie Watt

Ten Little Rabbits
    by Virginia Grossman & Sylvia Long

Ten Monkey Jamboree
    by Dianne Ochiltree & Anne-Sophie Lanquetin

Wanda's Washing Machine
    By Anna McQuinn & Jan McCafferty

When I Grow Up
    by P.K. Hallinan

Suggested Readings for Daddy

Father's Day by Bill McCoy, Random House

Parenting Your 1- to 4-Year-Old by Michael H.
    Popkin, PhD, Active Parenting Publishers

Pregnant Fathers by Jack Heinowitz, PhD, Parents as
    Partners Press

Road to Fatherhood by Jon Morris,
    Morning Glory Press, Inc.

*The Expectant Father: Facts, Tips & Advice for Dads-
    to-Be,* Second Edition by Armin Brott and
    Jennifer Ash

The New Father: A Dad's Guide to the First Year
    Second Edition by Armin Brott

The New Father's Panic Book by Gene William, Avon
    Books

*What Are My Rights? 95 Questions and Answers
    About Teens and the Law* by Thomas Jacobs,
    et. al., Free Spirit Publishing

Children's Nursery Rhymes

Your child will love to hear you sing songs and repeat rhymes—an important tool for language and literacy development. You can sing nursery rhymes while feeding your child, riding in the car, waiting at the doctor's office, during bath time or while taking a walk.

Little Bo-Peep

Little Bo-Peep has lost her sheep,
And can't tell where to find them.
Leave them along, and they'll come home,
Wagging their tales behind them.

Simple Simon

Simple Simon met a pieman,
Going to the fair.
Says Simple Simon to the pieman,
"Let me taste your ware."

Jack and Jill

Jack and Jill went up the hill,
To fetch a pail of water.
Jacke fell down, and broke his crown,
And Jill came tumbling after.

Jack Be Nimble

Jack be nimble,
Jack be quick,
Jack jump over the candlestick.

Pease Porridge

Pease porridge hot,
Pease porridge cold,
Pease porridge in the pot,
Nine days old.

Some like it hot,
Some like it cold,
Some like it in the pot,
Nine days old.

Old Mother Hubbard

Old Mother Hubbard went to the cupboard,
To get her poor dog a bone.
But when she got there
The cupboard was bare,
And so the poor dog had none.

Hey Diddle, Diddle

Hey diddle, diddle!
The cat and the fiddle,
The cow jumped over the moon.
The little dog laughed.
To see such sport,
And the dish ran away with the spoon.

Little Boy Blue

Little Boy Blue, come blow your horn!
The sheep's in the meadow,
The cow's in the corn.
Where's the little boy that
Looks after the sheep?
Under the haystack, fast asleep!

Miss Muffett

Little Miss Muffet sat on a tuffet,
Eating her curds and whey.
There came a big spider,
That sat down beside her,
And frightened Miss Muffet away.

Humpty Dumpty

Humpty Dumpty sat on a wall,
Humpty Dumpty had a great fall.
All the King's horses, and
All the King's men,
Couldn't put Humpty together again.

The Muffin Man

Oh, do you know the muffin man,
The muffin man, the muffin man?
Oh, do you know the muffin man
That lives in Drury Lane?

Oh, yes, I know the muffin man,
The muffin man, the muffin man.
Oh, yes, I know the muffin man
That lives in Drury Lane.

Activity Recipes

Have some fun with your toddler! A great idea for a cloudy or cold day is to work together to make these recipes and then play with the product. Don't forget to add protective coverings for surfaces. Maybe have your toddler wear one of your old shirts to protect their clothing.

Goop

Pour one box (16 oz.) of cornstarch into a bowl. Add water, a little at a time, to the dry cornstarch. Ask your toddler to help mix the cornstarch and water together until the ingredients form "goop."

Put the mixture onto a cookie sheet and use to form shapes and objects.

Peanut Butter Dough

1 cup peanut butter
1 cup nonfat dry milk

Mix together, adding more peanut butter or milk until you have the consistency you desire. This dough is edible.

Finger Paint

Combine 2 cups flour and 4 cups water in a small sauce pan. Stir over low heat until thickened. Add a pinch of salt and mix in food coloring. Cool and store in a covered container in the refrigerator.

Cinnamon Dough (for ornaments)

1 Tablespoon all spice
1 Tablespoon nutmeg
¾ cup cinnamon
2 Tablespoons ground cloves
1 cup applesauce

Mix ingredients in a large bowl. To use, roll out dough and cut with cookie cutters. Poke a hole at the top of each shape. Place shapes on a baking sheet covered with waxed paper. Air dry for several days, turning often.

__Journal Page__
Today, I will _____
in order to feel fulfilled.
DATE_____

_____
_____
_____
_____
_____
_____
_____
_____
_____
_____
_____
_____
_____
_____
_____
_____
_____
_____
_____
_____
_____
_____
_____
_____
_____
_____
_____

Index

About the Author

Juliann Galmarini Mangino, Ed.D. has served as a counselor and life coach for teen parents for more than a decade. While working full-time as a life coach, Juliann received her doctorate degree from the University of Pittsburgh. Her doctoral dissertation, *Voices of Teen Mothers: Their Challenges, Support Systems and Successes,* explored the skills and character traits that helped keep teen parents in high school and achieve graduation.

ABCs for Daddy! is Juliann's second book in her *Young Parenting Series*. Her first book, *ABCs for Mommy!* has been enthusiastically received and has sold thousands of copies nationwide.

Juliann earned a Masters in Counseling Education K-12 from Westminster College in New Wilmington, Pennsylvania and Bachelor of Arts in Education from Slippery Rock University in Slippery Rock, Pennsylvania.

Every day Juliann works hard to practice what she preaches. She, along with her husband, enthusiastically—and sometimes successfully—attempt to model positive character traits for their 12-year-old twins.

9 780615 582184